Dreams Create Endless Possibilities

Poetry, Prose, & Affirmations

Bobbie Moore-Howard

LET'S RETHINK THAT
Atlanta, GA
www.letsrethinkthat.com

Erica   3/16/19

You are A Beautiful child
of the most high God.
Remember that Love conquers
all and love never fails.
Always walk in love, peace
And Joy today + forever.
Just Be your authentic self
And believe that you are so
very special. God loves
You much more than you
Will ever Know.
Love

Bobbie Moore-Howard

Bobbie Moore-Howard
bmoorehoward@bellsouth.net

Dedication

Your heavenly Father loves you and He cares for all that concerns you. Remember who you are in Christ and know you are worthy. Earline would call me when I lived in New York and now living in Georgia to ask me to write a poem for various family gatherings. Over the years, I would call to get her opinion on the words and she would always say that's good and so perfect for the occasion. She would mention to me from time to time that you are a writer, you should write. I began to remember what I have once forgotten to be true to my gift and walk in my destiny. I want to say that life is a journey and not a destination, ever learning and being refreshed with new knowledge. Please stop hoping for the mediocre and began to dream big again. My desire for you is to be appreciative for everything in your life. Annie would always say, just tell the Lord thank you. She at times sends thought for the day to encourage us. I'm believing for you and myself to simply have an attitude of gratitude. Invite the Holy Spirit to be a part of all the decisions in your life. Just say daily, I expect good things to happen to me and through me. When you dedicate yourself to helping others, God will surely help you. Please know that you are truly valued also precious in His sight and is of great worth.

Love - Peace - Joy - And - Have - Faith - To - Believe

Acknowledgements

I thank you almighty God for my life, health, and strength. I am humbled and eternally grateful for keeping me in perfect peace. I have faith and trust as I began to truly dream again.

Thanks to my beautiful daughter Jennifer for your devotion, unconditional love and all your support, saying you got this.

Thanks to my grandson Brandon Jr. that I call my little grand man. You bring much love, peace, joy, and laughter in my life.

Family and Friends

I appreciate how you encouraged me in all the good and the difficult times. I am grateful that we do believe in each other.

I am grateful to Latanya for reminding me that the power is within me. It can be done but I must truly remain focused.

Thanks to Dr. Derrick Tennial (Let's REThink That Literary Services) for your expertise, love, time, and patience. I'm calling you the closer of this special project.

Thanks to my Spirit and Truth Family which is special to me. I appreciate Pastors D.E. & Brandi Paulk also Pastors Don & Clariece Paulk for prayers, teaching and labor of love. You teach truth and that the power is definitely within us.

Thanks to Bishop Carlton Pearson for all your love and teachings graciously including everyone in all walks of life.

Foreword

D.E. Paulk

In Dreams Create Endless Possibilities, Bobbie Moore-Howard teaches, encourages, exhorts, challenges, and most importantly inspires all who read it to recognize the power within themselves and to dream endless dreams of possibility for their lives. As her pastor, I can truly say that Bobbie lives what she writes and practices the principles set forth in her stunningly beautiful poetry and prose.

As you read, take Bobbie's own words to heart:

> *"Get Up Now*
> *Go Do Something*
> *Move Forward*
> *Don't Just Sit There*
> *Dream It – Say It – Write It – Act on It*
> *You must truly be in it, to courageously win it!"*

D.E. Paulk is the Senior Pastor of Spirit and Truth Sanctuary, a thriving multicultural, interfaith, LGBTQIA affirming congregation in Atlanta, Georgia. D.E is widely known as a radically inclusive minister of reconciliation who believes that the Christ spirit is present in all of creation and cannot be defined by, nor confined to, Christianity.

Foreword

Jennifer Howard Riley

When I look over the years, I remember watching my mother always writing something on paper. She made note of any and everything happening around us. If a family member was in the hospital, she kept record of their progress (as well as the medical staff with whom she developed a relationship) during their hospital stay. She wrote words of encouragement for family and friends for birthdays, anniversaries, and the loss of loved ones. She noted all my achievements in childhood and my accomplishments as a young adult. Now she has even started documenting every moment of the life of my son - Brandon, Jr. – and he is only three years old. I would at times say to her, "You're always writing; you need to write a book."

Her first book, Dreams Create Endless Possibilities, is a book that features poetry, prose, and affirmations about renewing your mind and dreaming again. Reading this book reminded me that my mother is an encourager who desires for everyone to live purpose-filled lives, knowing that we are blessed, highly favored, and not deprived of anything! Through each poem, she reminds us that the power is within and that God, our source, does not need anyone's approval or permission to bless us. Walk with my mother on her new journey and believe that dreams do create endless possibilities. Dream big again, always strive for excellence, and walk in your destiny.

Table of Contents

Categories

Introduction

Lord, You are my strength as I rest in the Shadow of your Wings. I feel so loved and safe as I'm resting in your loving arms. I sometimes feel the need to just sit and rest in the palm of your hands where there is safety and complete peace. I am so delighted knowing that when my eyes were not yet opened to spirit and truth, you were there. As I began to read the word and study for myself with very little clarity, you were there. I realized that I was in a low-level of consciousness, unaware of how special and whose I am. As time passed and the days and months just seem to drift away from me, you were there. When I began to move forward, situations and circumstances just happens. Truly my eyes are opened to spirit and truth, my mind is renewed and is navigated by the Holy Spirit. I now strive to live on a much higher plane and with no more negativity. Life is about choices which results in rewards or consequences. I am learning that my spirit is lining up with the spirit of Christ each day. I am walking along the path that is destined, especially for me, learning to create my very own possibilities. I just watch and pray, continue to stay in faith as my new life unfolds. If I am not happy with my life, I can turn the page, dream again, and recreate. Come walk with me and enjoy the journey.

Everything in Love

Affirmations

Anoint You to Be

The most valued relationship in your life
Having the Holy Spirit as a Team Mate no strife
Your wrong decisions will eventually find you out
When you least suspect while you are out and about
Be true to yourself as time passes each and every day
Take off the mask unveil just be real in every way
If you choose to live in the anointing that gives true
substance to the relationship
Connect with people in a non-judging way now that's
called friendship
Express emotions to show that you are all there
Listen intensely to let that person know you really care
If you want a friend you must show yourself friendly I
must say
Trust that you are anointed to keep peace in your day
Not to worry about what others might think of you
The Holy Spirit will truly inspire what you must do
Be yourself, stay grateful, and keep love in your heart
Live your life be happy and just simply do your part
Always strive to keep love peace and joy in your day
As the anointing guides, all will be revealed in every way

Now He who establishes us with you in Christ and has anointed us to God.

II Corinthians 1:21

Blessed and Highly Favored

Remember who you are in Christ my precious child
Know that God cares whether you're loud or meek and mild
You have been abundantly blessed so many times in the past
Oh of course knowing that only what you do for Christ will last
You are awesomely blessed and so powerfully loved today
Trust in that inner small voice and let faith and peace have its way
You are sitting in the Palm of God's Hand today and forever more
You are a Child of the King you set the stage and definitely have the floor
Walk into your Destiny and vast in all God's glory and favor toward you
Bless others in your path never judge show mercy and simply hold true
When God gives you any heavenly or earthly treasures or any good thing
Take the time to share with others and give praises to God our King
I am blessed and highly favored more than I could ever ask or think today
You are blessed supernaturally as well and all is wonderful in every way
Remember to be kind and willing to help others and love long
Keep peace in your day especially joy in your life you can't go wrong
Remember what you make happen for others God will make happen for you
Continue to walk in the blessings of God and all His wonderful favor too
When you know whose you are and seem to just know where you are going
Life is much sweeter and the blessings of God just seem to keep flowing
I know that I am a child of The King in my body mind and my soul
Just living my life daily simply watching the love of God creatively unfold
You and I are precious vessels Of God and caregivers in this great land
We need to be grateful and to make known that we do care and understand
Never take the favor of God and His tender mercy for granted you see
He will always provide and share His goodness toward you and me
Rest in the grace of God and hold onto the strength and peace there
All is well with you knowing that God is love and He does care

I will make you a great nation, I will bless you and make your name great
and you shall be a blessing.

Genesis 12:2

Love in Everything

Love is being happy
Learn to laugh, dance and simply enjoy your life
Love is in a dream shared
Simply ponder in your heart and breathe life into it
Love is not bondage
Just began to walk in power and live in freedom
Love is in your hand
Just simply reach out to someone and gently touch
Love is in your heart
Share the love of God and spread wherever you go
Love is filled with joy
Always know that the joy of the Lord is your strength
Love is in a smile
Always keep a cheerful expression on your face
Love is the Trinity
Three-fold cord the Father, Son, and the Holy Spirit
Love is thinking of others
Remember to just be generous and kind to someone
Love Is being your best self
Just began to be creative and show love in everything

Beloved, if God so loved us, we also ought to love one another.

I John 4:11

And above all things have fervent love for one another, for love will cover a multitude of sins.

I Peter 4:8

The Power of You

I am truly amazed at what I can sometimes do
My life has been so enriched because of you
The Holy Spirit has come to help lead and guide me
I just continue to improve and get better you see
Life is so beautiful once your eyes are opened
Hold your tongue be silent because God has spoken
You can now see life through clean and clear glass
The fog and clouds are gone no more colorful past
God sent His Son to give His life so many years ago
We are facing reality that we can walk through any door
Knowing the race through Him has already been won
You and I positively with no doubt can carry on
When circumstances seem to be getting the best of you
Expect only the good and faith will carry you through
When you think you are alone and feel out of control
The Holy Spirit will give you the strength to take hold

Now to Him who is able to do exceedingly abundantly above all that we ask or think according to the power that works in us.

Ephesians 3:20

You Are The Great I Am

You Are   -   Beautiful in His sight
Look at God, there is absolutely none greater than you
You Are   -   Cheerful Giver
A generous person and always with a smile on your face
You Are   -   Child of the King
That makes you special never worry what others think
 You Are   -   Growing more in grace
Here a little there a little like watching a flower grow
You Are   -   Made in God's own image
Look in the mirror at yourself and see just how divine
You Are   -   Spiritual Being
So there is simply nothing natural or ordinary about you
You Are   -   The Great I AM
Meaning you can do all things through Christ's strength
You Are   -   Worshiper
Believe you are recognized and known by your praise

I am now learning that the power is not in You Are, but in I AM.
Read these words once more, change the words (You Are to I AM.)
Remember you and I have the power, so by all means embrace it.

Also do not take to heart everything people say, lest you hear your servant cursing you.

Ecclesiastes 7:21

Come Walk with Me

Poetic Expressions and Prose

A Blessed Child of God

A child is a true and perfect gift from God
Parents please never yield or spare the rod
Train your child during their early years
Trust and avoid some future pain and tears
Grasping as a child is a slow yet rapid process
Believe for the wonder and their great success
Your child's mind is like a sponge,
absorbing knowledge in and out of the classroom

Life is so amazing such mysteries no place for gloom
That child is simply enjoying the playground
Can only see the positive just look all around
Parents stay in Covenant with God always
It will be a blessing throughout their days
Parents never hold back that child's correction
It is positively for their very own protection

And all thy children shall be taught of the Lord; and great shall be the peace
of thy children.

Isaiah 54:13

13

Always Learning and Never Doubt

When you truly began to learn who you are
Striving for excellence to reach the top of the scale its highest bar
When you are fighting a battle always aim to win
The power within you states that you will not break nor bend
Keep in mind there is no enemy that can manipulate or defeat you
That will happen if you give away your power read and rightfully divide
the word of truth whatever you do
Sometimes you have to step completely out of your comfort zone
Walk never doubt in your heart move forward have faith knowing
You are not alone

I know that you are a true and quite an awesome God all the time
Yes, with your strength I can peacefully walk and have a sound mind
When you decide to step up and assert yourself be strong and above all
continue to stand tall

Have faith to believe and continue to trust God through it all
Yes, strive to be the best that you can in every way
Leaning and depending on the Holy Spirit throughout your day
Here a little and there a little simply line upon on line
Sing His praises and keep a song in your heart all the time

Oh God, you are more awesome than your Holy places. The God of Israel
is He who gives strength and power to His people.

Psalm 68:35

As You Strive to Live

As you Activate
Just being an active part of your own everyday life
As you Believe
Believe all is well and receive the promises of God
As you Communicate
Keep talking with your Father and the Holy Spirit
As you are Determined
Just stay focused and continue to live your best life
As you live in Expectation
Daily anticipate and Expect good things to happen
to you and through you
As You have Faith
Always have faith to accomplish whatever you desire
As You grow in Grace
Here a little and there a little also line upon line
As you live and Love
Please know that love does prevail and conquers all
As you remain Standing
When all else fails stand and endure to the very end
As you continue to Walk
Walking all along the path that is paved just for you

For you have need of endurance, so that after you have done the will of God, you may receive the promise.

Hebrews 10:36

15

Be in Covenant

God can relate to family starting with Adam and Eve
Do not betray God just trust and never to deceive
Covenant is shelter from the storm it is strength just
simply being apart

Covenant is togetherness and loving from the heart
Church is a refuge for all different types of people
It is not just a building designed with a tall steeple
Repentance moves from Kingdom of darkness to light
Caring for one another just truly love day and night
The highway to joy is through God's correction
Always remember Covenant demands God's protection
Discernment teaches you levels of right and wrong
Meditate be faithful keep in your heart a praise song
Trust the power within you for all divine provisions
Covenant keeps you in a perfect state of mind to make
the right decisions

Having inner peace knowing that the answer to all that concern
you is certainly inside

Stay in Covenant and continue to keep the faith true love you
cannot hide

If your sons will keep my covenant and My testimony which I shall teach
them. Their sons also shall sit upon your throne forever.

Psalm 132:12

Believe in You

You must of course have faith and believe in yourself
Do not put how you feel or your thoughts on a shelf
You must believe and have faith in the new and creative you
Trust in your higher self and never say what you cannot do
You must believe in the yet new possibilities and your own ideas
Never feel that other people know what's best for you or shed tears
You must continue to believe at all cost in your very own potential
Definitely do not think of yourself in any way as a non-essential
You must believe that receiving God's best is yet to come in your life
No more self-doubt you are equipped to accomplish without strife
You must believe that you have the spirit of Christ within you today
Open your eyes look around at the beauty embrace it in every way
You must believe and know that you are made in God's own image
Never lose hope you are a part of the Household of Faith Lineage
You must believe in the divine power that resides within you
Search your heart the answer is in your routine the things you do
You must believe in your success a creative thought in your mind
Think and re-think about your everyday habits of any kind
Go somewhere and sit down in your closet that quiet place
Renew your mind stay in peace and keep a smile on your face
You must begin to believe in all the good things concerning you
Believe in yourself the best is yet to come in whatever you do

---

But these are written that you may believe that Jesus is the Christ the Son
of God and that believing you may have life in His name.

John 20:31

17

Blessed to Be a Blessing

When you wake up each morning just simply say
Thank you Lord for my new opportunity today
Always have a grateful and a thankful attitude
Have a giving and loving spirit will determine your altitude

Say These Words Daily:
1. I Expect good things to happen to me today.
2. I Expect good things to happen through me today.

When there is a task that God placed in you to do
Do not fret with details, He will provide for you
But on the other hand, you should count the cost
Don't be overwhelmed in the process not confused or lost
Go on step out on the waters now and hold true
Trust and believe in the power that lives within you
Remember to think of others as you pass along
Just do the right thing, you cannot go wrong

I will make you a great nation, I will bless you and make your name great,
and you shall be a blessing.

Genesis 12:2

Brandi and Me

My Daughter in My Other Life

This is just a few lines to cheer you and just to make you smile or laugh. I realize you are not my biological daughter, but perhaps maybe in my other life. We have always been spiritually connected even when unaware. I constantly feel your presence in my spirit and I know that deep down you are my child. If you would look in the mirror and turn around and look at me, you'll see we are identical. (not laugh to hard)

You and I truly have beautiful voices, with such perfect vocal cords. We can just hit those high operatic notes on demand, so amazing. I'm so excited when I hear you sing unto the Lord. We are both computer experts but you are the genius in the family, just so knowledgeable in the IT field. If there is any technical difficulty with the computer or lap top you will correct the problem within a few minutes. Whatever we put our hands to, it is done and with sheer greatness and with high standards, that's how we live. (smile or laugh)

You have a great husband name D.E. who simply adore you and is a good Dad to your babies who are teenagers but still your babies. He is a wonderful man chosen by God just for you. You can just unmask and simply be Brandi with him. You can talk, discuss things, agree sometimes to disagree, and still love each other. You know, He calls you "My Brandi" and he says that he definitely married up. You and I certainly know that He is a Man of God that always speaks the truth. (smile)

You have a daughter and a son name Esther and Micah who are simply adorable and so talented. The apple does not fall far from the tree are shall I say trees. Both of your children have the potential of being a top professional athlete and musical masters or any career they choose. Their dad has multiple talents and is quite the athlete himself and coaches their games. Music and Art is definitely in their blood because of their Grandmother, the music and arts master in her own right. You know the sky is the limit because they are striving for excellence and they do have your DNA to strive and achieve. You dream it, speak it, act on it and it is done. They are Spiritual Beings living a Natural Experience. Remember whatever they are going toward in life, God is there in the midst of it all. (smile)

Oh, when you and I sang the Anthem at the High School Basketball Game, we were wonderful. I must say that the people simply loved us. I had a flash back of my past fame and fortune. When I see you, I feel re-incarnated from my glorious and glamorous past. Remember you are special and uniquely made. There is only one like you (Me). Keep in mind when there is no mirror available, just look at me. Just Knowing who you are is truly essential. I wish that all your desires are granted and is lined up with the Spirit. (smile)

As a result, when the smiles and the laughter has ceased temporarily for now. I just want you to know that you are truly a Child of the King. Please know that you will not be deprived of any good thing. You chose to dream big and definitely acted on it. You have successfully achieved your goals and is still striving and demanding the best life for you and your family. When the dust has settled, please remember You Are absolutely the gracious I Am indeed.

Yes, I do have a beautiful, intelligent biological daughter name Jennifer, but in my heart I am a mother of two. (smile)

Many daughters have done well but you excel them all.

Proverbs 31:29

Learn from It and Simply Embrace

Sometimes negative things happen in our lives you know
Keep the faith, by all means, never let the fear show
When you feel that you have been dropped a time or two
Have faith to believe, get up, stand tall and began anew
When you feel mistreated and very much misunderstood
Think positive, recreate, and know that life can be good
God knows what is going on in your life right now
Have patience and allow the Holy Spirit to work, wow
Keep a positive attitude and seek to learn all you can
Trust in the power within you knowing that God has a plan
There are times you must be still, get quiet to hear from God
When you are awake and committed, it's not that hard
After all that has happened, look around you're still here
Thank you, God, now I can hear loud and very clear
Sometimes the people that you expect to be there for you
They are lost in their own afflictions their hands are tied too
Remember when different changes, negative or positive come
your way
Stand strong and ask yourself what is the lesson that I should be
learning from this today

Keep in mind that Changes come and changes go
Learn and embrace it and let the positive expressions flow.

This is my comfort in my affliction, For Your word has given me life.

Psalm 119:50

21

Contentious Woman

Change your Attitude and Live a Happy Life

A Contentious Woman is similar to a rain drop
She goes on and on never knowing when to stop
Can you imagine water that goes drip, drip, drip all the time?
Her disposition is enough to drive her husband out of His mind
Somehow you must know that life must change along the way
You need help and God's word in the midst of each and every day
Stop and just look in the mirror again and again at yourself
Put your nagging and bad attitude up high on the tallest shelf
Ask the Holy Spirit to grant wisdom to lead and guide you
Trust God to give you the mind to change the things that you do
As the days began to move on and you start seeing the light
Life looks better, day approaching the sun does shine bright
Began to take another look in the mirror with a renewed mind
Oh, my God such a transformation and you look so divine
Just began to thank God for the new and improved you
Just have faith to believe and keep love in everything you do

---

Better to dwell in the wilderness, than in a house shared with a contentious
and angry woman.

Proverbs 21:19

22

Dad, Our Letter to You

Russell Moore Sr.

You will be remembered as a quiet, humble, peaceful yet gentle man
But there were times you had to take a firm stand (7 children)
As we grew and became adults, we knew how to budget our money,
save and pay our bills on time
You saved jars filled with coins, we had easy access, the true
meaning of can you spare a dime
We learned to respect ourselves and others, also to show
kindness at an early age
You worked tirelessly for your family and others, you truly did
set the stage
Growing up, we watched you give, share constantly doing
good things everyday
You taught us to challenge ourselves and to always do our very
best in every way
Dad, as we attempt to close this letter which is hard to do
We decided not to say goodbye because we are your living fruit and
will forever continue your legacy too
We are an extension of your powerful and loving tree
The essence of you Dad, will live on in us for all to see
You just loved people and always gave simply from your heart
My siblings and I are grateful for all you have instilled in us
and just being a part

Children, Children are the crown of old men and the glory of children is their Father.

Proverbs 17:6

I and my Father are one.

John 10:30

Demand the Best Life

Do not hang with people who are negative in every way
Associate yourself with those who are positive everyday
Stop being manipulated always at their beckoning call
Feeling drained and all alone when you tumble or fall
Be very selective when you are choosing your friends
Know that some of them will not be with you to the end
There are times you have to walk away from your past
Make the best choice to live a positive future at last
Began to simply move forward with a renewed mind
Please look ahead and take heed to that big stop sign
Change your strategy dream again and live a good life
Turn the page recreate with no more confusion or strife
Wash away all that dirt and grime simply take a bath
Move forward stay on that straight and narrow path
Think again with a higher level of consciousness
Live your life with all its blessings and righteousness
Be very thankful and grateful as only you could
The best life is in store for you and all that is good

But earnestly desire the best gifts. And yet I show you a more excellent way.

I Corinthians 12:31

Destiny Seed

Please know Destiny Seed is locked into your DNA
Trust in yourself, that inner spirit to find your way
Destiny Gene does not come from Natural heritage you see
It comes from God the Father which lives inside you and me
Ministry is already apart of you, unaware at an early age
Discovering hidden treasures will prepare you for life's stage
Remember you are the seed of Abraham please never forget
As you grow, knowing that God is not through with you yet
Breathe life into your DNA according to the promises of God
As you began to walk toward spirit and truth it's not so hard
What you can't see is lying still and quite dormant inside you
God will place people in your path to help guide you too
Sometimes He will allow you to stumble as you explore
Other times the spirit will say stop, don't, please no more
There is no failure in what God will instruct you to do
Have faith and trust, He will find a way to provide for you
Keep walking toward the light and see the beauty all around
Trust in your potential and your true greatness will abound
Remember, you are more than just an average woman or man
Believing in your higher self, heir to the throne, now that is
God's Master Plan

If you belong to Christ, then you are Abraham's seed, and heirs according to the promise.

Galatians 3:29

Double Minded Man

Absolutely No Stability

A Double minded person is unstable in all His or Her ways
That type of person is so confused throughout their days
Things and thoughts might begin to creep into your head
Stay positive do not allow the negative to stay there and make a bed
You are aware of good and evil that surrounds you in the world
Try to focus on the good please see it as quite a wisdom pearl
You are at Church praising the Lord singing and raising your hand
On the parking lot, you were rude with the Parking Attendant Woman
You were really acting out of character everyone could hear and see
What happen to praise and worship who you were portraying to be
Please be careful what you say because others can certainly hear
What you say and speak will spread all around in the atmosphere
You are trying to be all things to all people that is dual personality
You need love peace and of course joy to simply face real spirituality
Live your life and not just in the moment please just be you
Stop living in a subconscious state trying to portray yourself as two
So trust God and take off the mask and renew your mind now
Have faith in God and the power within you to show you how
Remember everything you need is already living inside you
Trust the Holy Spirit for guidance and wisdom to know what to do

He is a double minded man unstable in all His ways.

James 1:8

Dreams and Visions

When you lay down and fall asleep in bed at night
Sometimes you have a dream that causes a great fright
We called that a terrible or an awful nightmare
Something you really do not want to remember or share
When you fall into a deep sleep and began to dream
You toss and turn in bed, it appears so real it seems
If you could just write it down and make it plain
Dwell on the positive, allowing only the good things to emerge and remain
Write the vision, know there is a level of accountability
You are responsible for your own productivity and availability
Identify anything or anyone trying to block your view
Step away from those circumstances or people not letting you be you
If that situation causes you to lose your vision
Rethink and regroup, just began to start on a new and exciting revision
If that person is definitely not at the level where you are
Just want you to simply forget about your dreams, now that's going much
to far

In a dream, in a vision of the night. When deep sleep falls upon men.

Job 33:15

Dreams and Visions – Never Stop

Dreams and Visions should always be a part of your life
Keep a fresh and a new thought in your heart, no strife
As you began to eat of the word and feel so nourished
Your mind will be open to the things of God and you
will begin to flourish
Do not let any negative thought get inside of you
Remain, oh so positive in everything that you do

Get yourself a Vision Board, whether you are young or old
Be creative, live your life, just began to imagine, and be bold

Get Up Now   Go Do Something   Today
Move Forward   Don't Just Sit There   Do It Now

Dream It - Say It - See It - Write It - Act on It
Rejoice in it - Enjoy it

You must truly be in it, to courageously win It

In a dream, in a vision of the night. When deep sleep falls upon men.
Job 33:15

Then the Lord answered me and said: write the vision and make it plain on tablets, that He may run who reads it.
Habakkuk 2:2

Encourage Others and Have Courage

Remember whose you are and keep your mind clear
Listen to that inner small voice very close in your ear
Please know there is nothing that is too hard for God
As you continue to travel in your life, an uphill trod
There's a little shaking in the camp all around you
Your Angels are hovering and know just what to do
Believe that No hurt, harm or danger will come near
There is no need to worry nor feel sad or live in fear
Stay strong and be of good cheer, have faith and say
God will help you make it through each and everyday
Get ready, your breakthrough is on its way real soon
Always stay in peace and began to sing a new tune
When your life is not the way you imagined or planned
Continue to trust and believe, above all take a stand
When there is no one around to lift or encourage you
Get up encourage yourself stand strong and hold true

In Courage- Means to inspire with courage and spirit or confidence.
It absolutely takes courage- To speak life to someone.
You must have courage-To attempt to encourage others.

That is that I may be encouraged together with you by the mutual faith
both of you and me.

Roman I:12

Ever Thankful

Such an Attitude

Find things to be thankful for in your life
Just had an awful past entirely too much strife
You might have been mistreated and maybe abused
Step away from people who make you feel misused
Be humble ever thankful in spite of how you feel
Think of the good things, trust in God, do His will
Turn your pain into something positive you see
Please stop the negative and simply let it be
Learn to be more assertive and aggressive
You will later turn your mess into your message
You no longer have to live oh so defeated
Begin to be transformed, yes laugh, and repeat it
There are mishaps in our lives we just can't control
As life changes, make better choices and be bold
You will feel lifted and maintain a thankful attitude
Your attitude in life will determine your altitude
Believe in yourself, cease from being critical and not complain
Have faith, only what you do for Christ will remain

Humble yourselves in the sight of the Lord and He will lift you up.

James 4:10

Every Day "Teach"

You listen to the Holy spirit, truly a God's Man
Willing to get quiet and hear God's voice and take that unpopular stand
You were born to be a fore runner and a lead domino
You are on a path and have followed your destiny and is
letting your light show
As you continue to lead the way, angels are peaceably camped all
around you
Goodness and mercy shall always consistently just seem to follow you too
You will be blessed and strengthen today and always
Your eyes are opened and you will remain awake and committed
throughout your days
You have taught us and everyone around you to read the Bible
and rightly divide
Ask the Holy Spirit to give us such clarity that we can hold
onto and not hide
Thank you for spiritual guidance and helping us to see
We really appreciate all your love and concern for us
Pastor D. E.

And my speech and my preaching were not with persuasive words of human
wisdom. But in demonstration of the spirit and of power.

I Corinthians 2:4

Faith to Believe

Lean not to your own understanding
Life can be difficult and very demanding
Faith is the unseen, you must believe
Trust God an abundant life you will receive
When things in life do not look the way they should
Believe all things will work together for your good
Know that in God, you must hold fast and certainly be awake
Life can sometimes be a little hard, but you will not bend nor break
Continue to live your life the best that you can each and everyday
Trust that Spirit and Truth will lead and guide you all along the way
As you walk along the path that is set before you
Keep moving forward, stay focused in all that you are destined to do.
Have faith to believe in all that is truly good
Trust and live your best life as only you should
When they go low, you must go high and rise above
Look up and soar like a gracious flying white dove

Now faith is the substance of things hoped for, the evidence of things not seen.

Hebrews 11:1

And we know that all things work together for good to those who love God, to those who are called according to His purpose.

Roman 8:28

Together Stand Strong

Once upon a time there was a Husband and a Wife
Later an addition of a newly born Baby, God's gift to your life
Becoming parents, that little life, depends strictly on you
Be careful because that child will watch all that you do
Be a role model that your child can rely on and truly follow
Trust and never bite off more than you can chew or swallow
Sometimes life can be complicated and not what it seems
Be there to teach Him or Her to surely have high self esteem
Teach your Child that life is compared to running a race
Train that child to walk, run to endure and keep up the pace
Father provoke not your child never cause anger or strife
Mother, reveal to your child to love and have a peaceful life
Please believe that the power is certainly within you
Have faith knowing that the spirit will bring you through
Being a part of a loving family is special and so essential
Loving each other at all cost, gives the family such potential
There is covenant between us and love will conquer all
When family is so close and strong, you can stand quite tall

But God has revealed them to us through His spirit. For the Spirit searches all things, yes, the deep things of God.

I Corinthians 2:10

Train up a child in the way He should go. And when he is old he will not depart from it.

Proverbs 22:6

Finishing Grace

I was not created to quit anything in my life
I was created to complete and finished without strife
I will stand strong not back down to anyone you see
Life is very unpredictable just simply step away from me
The love of God helps me to feel so powerful in all
I strive to do
Knowing who you are in Christ pushes you into your
destiny simply hold true
Do not let anyone attempt to validate you at any cost
You are a spiritual being never feel less than or lost
The Lord have you and I in the palm of His hand
Get up move forward keep creating and make a stand
Quitting is not in your vocabulary stay on your path
Know your heavenly Father is working on your behalf
You must have finishing grace never think of giving up
Run your race endure to the end to receive that shiny
winner's cup

For by grace you have been saved through faith, and that not of yourselves;
It is the gift of God.

Ephesians 2:8

Forgiveness Is So Essential

To forgive is not necessarily an option in your life
Forgiveness is really for you to remove any and all strife
Please do not hold any confusion or malice in your heart
To forgive is divine and search for a fulfilling new start
As you walk the narrow path, continue to renew your mind
Live in the present and just simply put the past behind
Showing kindness is so essential not at all hard to do
When you are affected by difficult times, please hold true.
To forgive is attempting to walk in the other person's shoes
In the midst of hostility, you do not want to feel abused
Remember all the love and mercy shown toward you
Yes, forget all the bad and stop feeling less than or blue
Hear these profound words, life can be rewarding you see
Learn to accept that long and overdue apology you will
        never get in the natural, just let it be
When you genuinely forgive in all aspects of your life today
You will find yourself happy and at peace in every way
Remember to always think of the other person's feelings
        before you began to speak
Having a forgiving heart is what you should always seek

For you, Lord, are good, and ready to forgive. And abundantly in mercy to all those who call upon you.

Psalm 86:5

Fruit of the Spirit

Fruit of the Spirit
Apart of your inner being
Love
Conquers all and prevails, always keep in your heart
Joy
Is above emotions, happiness, always keep in your life
Peace
Is a state of mind, be calm, always keep in your day
Longsuffering
Is patient and endures to the end, will keep you humble
Kindness
Think of others as God have shown mercy toward us
Goodness
Shall follow you all of your life and leads to repentance
Faithfulness
Surrounds you, endures to all generation and it abides
Gentleness
Bearing one another in love, unity in spirit and always
pursue righteousness
Self-Control
Is perseverance, true Godliness, be sober minded, be
hospitable to others and love what is good

But the fruit of the Spirit is love, joy, peace, longsuffering, kindness, goodness, faithfulness, gentleness, self-control, against such there is no law.

Galatians 5:22-23

Getting Together

Think Before You Say I Do

Getting together is a very important step in your life
Remember not to rush in without prayer and no strife
Get to know the other person to the best of your ability
You have to communicate and yet have some stability
Thinking of possibly becoming one is a very big decision
Search yourselves thoroughly to see if there is any division
Having the mind of Christ, the answer will come, just stand
Trust God and believe, the Holy Spirit is a part of your plan
If the thought of living your new life causes a little dismay
You realize that you need a little more time to think and pray
Please listen to that still small voice and keep a clear mind
Wait patiently for the answer, it might take a little more time
Getting married is an extremely big commitment to make
Remember there is no room for error or any mistake
Trust and believe and hold on to God's unchanging hand
He will guide you all along the way remain calm and stand
Go on with your life and simply do what you routinely do
The higher level of consciousness will prevail inside you

Trust in the Lord with all your heart and lean not to your own understanding.

Proverbs 3:5

In all your ways acknowledge Him, and He shall direct your paths.

Proverbs 3:6

Happy Third Birthday, Brandon Jr.

My Little Grand Man

Brandon please know that you are a bright and shining light in my life today
You are so much fun and you love all people big or small in every way
Your life is filled with all good things and more is yet to come you'll see
You simply love life and you just love to play jump and run all around me
When I look at your life just seem to get so much better all around
You of course enjoy The Wheels on the Bus that goes all over Town
You love The Five Little Ducks that went swimming one day
Oh yes, they did travel all over the Hills and Far Away
You are so athletic and Baseball just seem to be your Game
Yes, running a Home Run really seem to be your Aim
Oh, I almost forgot that you also love Paw Patrol they're so much fun
You know Chase is on the Case see you later because we got to run
I would like to say that your Mom and Dad is so Blessed to have a Son like you
Life as you know it is simply great because you adore and love them too
So, continue to be you Brandon (B.J.) and the changes that will come
I just want to remind you to just go ahead and laugh and sound the alarm
I celebrate You and I want to let you know that you are (three) years old today
I am such a proud Grand Mother watching you grow and flourish in every way

Please Remember to Always and Forever Keep

Love	In Your Tender Little Yet Big Heart
Peace	Of Your Great Mind in Your Day
Joy	Constantly in Your Life

Love Always,
Your Proud Grand Ma

Train up a child in the way he should go; even when he is old he will not depart from it.

Proverbs 22:6

I Am Not Deprived

God Is My Source

I am not Alone or Lonely
Yes, Jesus loves me He walks with me talks with Me tells me I am His own
I have my natural family and my spiritual family living around me
I am not Angry or Confused
Truly I am at peace and yes, my mind is very clear and without any hesitation
I am not Broke or Disgusted
Thank You, God, I am prosperous and I live in abundance because of You
I am not Depressed or Distressed
Just look at me and see the peace and the joy on my face and in my life
I am not Homeless or Uncomfortable
Thank God that I do have a roof over my head and I live in a goodly House
I am not Hungry or Thirsty
Just look around there is no lack of food in my cupboard or pantry
I am not in Lack or Without
There is no present need because God is and have always been my Source
I am not Low or Underneath
Instead, I am quite powerful, remember Jesus paid it all many years ago
I am not Sad or Depressed
The Holy Spirit lives within me, I'm so Happy knowing whose I am
I am not Sick or any Disease
Yes, I am healthy, wealthy and will continue to grow and strive
I am not Without Hope
Please know that I have faith to believe that all is well now and forever
I am not Without Questions
The answer is not always in my grasp; I ask in prayer, the Lord hears me
I am not Worried at All
Just keep in mind, there is no worries when you live in faith
Know that faith and worry cannot live comfortably in the same house

---

And whatever things you ask in prayer, believing you will receive.

Matthew 21:22

Invitation to Dine

Highly Recommended to All Daily
Special Menu: Psalm 34, Psalm 37, Psalm 91, and Psalm 119.

You are cordially invited to come and partake with me and my companion (Holy Spirit). Consider this to be more than just a snack, you will be sustained after this meal. Do not concern yourself if it is not all eaten in one day or at the time you dined. Remember there is such a thing called left overs, so take a doggy bag or simply a to-go-box home. Keep in mind that finishing your food the next day is quite okay. Expect an Evite (RSVP) to Dine soon. The selection is exquisite and quite a cuisine. If you say yes, you will grow in body, mind, and soul. You will be nourished and began to flourish in the things of God, you will feel more alive and awake.

Come Dine with Me and Enjoy the Feast
You can bring your spouse, friend, or family members.
Just add 1, 2 or more, there is no limit. All are welcomed there.

The Menu Consist of: Appetizers, Salads, Entrees, and Deserts

1. *All things work together for your good.   Roman 8:28*
2. *Bring all the tithes in the storehouse.   Malachi 3:10*
3. *Desires of your heart.   Psalms 37:4*
4. *Give and it shall be given to you.   Luke 6:38*
5. *God said, let us make man in our image. Genesis 1:26*

Journey with My Siblings

Quite an Adventure

Growing up with my Siblings was a great journey traveled, as an adult I will always cherish. Life was filled with ups and downs, happy and sad, we had to accept the good and the bad. We learned the art of caring, giving, loving, sharing, trusting, and always having each other's backs. We will remember forever.

The Best Siblings

Mamie was quiet and a little timid earlier in every way
Now strong in God, she will always say, enjoy your day
Lillie was not shy at all, little short was not very tall
She revealed later that she was the most favored of us all
Earline was mean, stood strong and a little stubborn too
She keeps the family in harmony an intercessor, who knew
Bobbie, stubborn but unique, the one in the middle you see
I'm so grateful to be a part of such a loving and terrific family
Johnny (transitioned) was very strong and was so respected
He was over six feet tall, yes, we were always quite protected
Annie was a little shy, tried to keep the peace, all the time
Encourager always have a good word and a Christ like mind
Russell Jr (Duke) just seem to have all the answers for us
He is always giving and sharing, simply doing what he must
I would not trade my childhood for all the tea in China
Began to reminisce on the good while sitting in my recliner

My family and I are joined together through Blood and God's great Love.

These things I command you. That you love one another.

John 15:17

41

Just Be Diligent

Learn to Simply Rest

Sometimes situations in your life may seem
a little uncomfortable, that's true
There is some stirring going on all around you
I am excited for what's about to happen in your life
Whoever is trying to block you just stay peaceful -no strife
You are being pushed into your destiny that's all
I will pray that you do not stumble or drop the ball
No one has the power to close or crack your door
Rise above it all knowing who you are and soar
You are diligently going about your Father's business
and clothe in spirituality
That makes you an asset and never a liability
Always remember that no one can stop the flow
Keep a smile on your face and maintain your glow

He who has a slack hand becomes poor. But the hand of the Diligent make rich.

Proverbs 10:4

Keep your heart with all diligence. For out of it springs the Issue of life.

Proverbs 4:23

Just Give

By All Means With a Smile

To succeed in life, you must be a cheerful giver
God is a Man who can and will certainly deliver
My God can and shall supply all of your needs
You can positively take that to the bank indeed
Live your life and never be afraid or hesitate giving
When you care and share, now that's surely good living
Before you came to Jesus, you were bankrupt, having nothing
Now being a Child of The King, you are being exposed to
Every good thing.

Activate It

Charge It

Spirit and Truth
Master Card

Deposit It

J 3:16 R 8:37 P 4:19 E 11:4
Good Thru Eternity

Take Advantage of this Card regularly
[Recommend Daily]

For God so loved the world that He gave His only begotten Son that whosoever believes in Him should not perish but have ever lasting life.

John 3:16

Yet in all these things we are more than conquerors through Him who loved us.

Romans 8:37

And my God shall supply all your need according to His riches in glory by Christ Jesus.

Philippians 4:19

He who observes the wind will not sow, And He who regards the clouds will not reap.

Ecclesiastes 11:4

Kindergarten Teacher

Great and Wonderful Beginning

You were a special person who taught my Child at the
Stone Mountain Christian School
She was taught so much and had to especially follow the
guidelines and all the rules
There were so many lessons to learn on how to behave in
and out of the classroom
Your appearance was meticulous and you were always so
refined and well groomed
I highly recommend you as an experienced teacher who
always explained in such explicit detail
You walked in the Spirit and you taught love would always
triumph and prevail
As a mother, I just seem to know what my child can do
As an educator, you could also see the potential too
There were times you had to truly be very strict and firm
Day after day and month after month, you continued to show
such kindness and great concern
I must admit as a Teacher you certainly did your part
You have given my Daughter and so many other children a
wonderful and a marvelous start
Be confident knowing you have done your absolute best
You have surely and graciously past the ultimate test

I will instruct you and teach you in the way you should go.

Psalms 32:8

44

Knowing Who You Are Is So Essential

Make up your mind to do what must be done
Live your life peaceably, knowing that you've only just begun
Do not be moved by circumstances that changes all around you
Believe and trust simply do what you have to
When you began to realize and know who you are today
Life will start to unfold before your very eyes without any delay
God will definitely be on time just wait and see
Continue to pray and live your life, the best is yet to be
As you attempt to walk through a particular door
Keep an attitude of gratitude while you continue to explore
You have traveled so much in the past, now it's time to settle down
It is a wonderful feeling knowing that you can live a good life in a
big city or in a small town
Keep the faith and believe that love is all around you
Listen to that still small voice stay in peace and hold true
Remember you can do all things through Christ who is all powerful
and continues to provide
Just rest in knowing that His love will always abide and you simply
cannot cover or hide

Behold you desire truth in the inward parts. And in the Hidden part you will make me to know wisdom.

Psalm 51:6

Lemons Do Make Lemonade

Taste can be bitter or it can sometimes be very sweet
If wrong choices are made by you, please do not repeat
When life does not turn out the way you hoped or planned
Remember to keep trusting in God and continue to stand
Stir up your life in a positive way absolutely keep it up
Simply choose not to drink from that awful bitter cup
Friends can disappoint you and will inevitably let you down
Just be happy simply encourage yourself no need to frown
Know who you are in Christ and keep moving forward
Strive for excellence stay focused continue to look toward
Life can change very quickly of course at any given time
Keep a song in your heart and only the good on your mind
When circumstances come and get a little hard to bear
Remember not to forget that God will always be there
Sometimes your plans are made to be altered or even broken
Just hold on to God's unchanging hand, He has spoken
Know that all is not lost and this is certainly not the end
Strive to reach for the top and above all aim to win
Life can be such a challenge so continue to run your race
Keep moving forward in and out of changes, at your own
        pace and definitely in your own space
Remember to learn from the bitter sweet of your past
Go ahead, live in the now, with all the beauty that will last

---

Oh, taste and see that the Lord is good; Blessed is the man who trusts in Him!
Psalm 34:8

Love of a Precious Life

Your Beautiful Baby

A Baby is quite a beautiful bundle of joy
Someone to love and care for and simply enjoy
Hold that baby close and always show affection
Hug and embrace always give comfort and protection
A mother's gentle hand and her tender touch
Is held in high regard and is valued so very much
A mother's warm smile in her little baby's face
Just make His or Her tiny heart just skip and race
Start expressing love, your child will show emotions
In return, your child will begin to show sweet devotion
Dad, teach God's word knowing that you truly care
Teach your little one to be strong and learn to share
A father's love for his child is so very hard to explain
The joy that he feels inside is so difficult to contain
Mom and Dad always give and constantly show love
Your baby will begin to fit snug like a rubber glove
You know rubber stretches, automatically bounces back
Just loving and being loved will truly pick up the slack

That Christ may dwell in your hearts through faith; that you being rooted and grounded in love.

Ephesians 3:17

Love, Peace, Joy

Keys to Success in Life

Love does by all means conquer all
It lifts you up when you stumble and sometimes fall
Love is really without envy and strife
Simply stay in peace and trust God throughout your life
Love of course never quit on you or fail
True love that is mixed with joy will always prevail
Love will never purposely cause pain
As you live your life there will sometimes be a little rain
Love says to please call and lean on me
I'll be there from the beginning to the end you will see
Love is continued strength for the weak
Keep your joy when you have reached your lowest peak
Love is always generous and oh so kind
It maintains such joy in your heart and peace of mind
Love is quiet and calm during a storm
It will keep you comfortable, cozy, quite safe, and warm
Love is the greatest gift ever given to you
Be happy, keep the faith, remain focused and hold true.

As the father loved me, I also have loved you, abide in my love.

John 15:9

These things I command you, that you love one another.

John 15:17

Main Character in Your Life

You

Knowing who you are in Christ that's half the battle
Keep your peace be focused and stay in the saddle
Search inside yourself make changes simply create
If that idea does not accomplish what you dreamed of
own up to it and of course re-create
Life is what you desire and want to make of it
Remember you are the main character so you definitely
and positively cannot quit
When you fail and decide to quit, that means you no
longer believe in you
Tear up that page into tiny little pieces, throw it away
and began to re-write something new
Must I remind you that you are the main character on
the Big Screen
Go out there, begin to face reality, and present yourself
well because you are in every scene
Remember life is but a stage, so renew your mind
because you are the star of the show
Be steadfast, So Lights, Camera, Action, Get Ready Go

Create in me a clean heart, Oh God, and renew a steadfast spirit within me.
Psalm 51:10

Mal-Nourished

Natural v. Spiritual

Please know that eating one meal on Sunday is not enough
If you are not eating daily, life can be a little rough
Lack of food can cause the body to break down and feel weak
You are not well and your health is at its lowest peak
Keep in mind that the body needs food and water to survive
It is so detrimental to you to just simply, stay alive
You must realize that the lack of food can cause sickness
Lack of God's word can really cause wickedness
When you are not eating healthy, properly as you should
You will just do wrong things because you could
If you are not focused on God and living upright today
You will start doing anything to have your way
Not enough oxygen to the brain can cause confusion
Not hearing God's word can cause an illusion
Lack of food and water can cause a serious disease
Lack of the word of God can cause dis-ease
Continue to eat naturally and healthy to be nourished
Always eat spiritually to grow and flourish

In His days the righteous shall flourish. And abundance of peace until the moon is no more.

Psalm 72:7

For no one ever hated His own flesh, but nourishes and cherishes it, just as the Lord does the church.

Ephesians 5:29

My Mom

Lillie Pearl Moore

Who carried me for nine months comfortably cradled,
and nourished in her womb
My Mom
Who took excellent care of me as an infant and called me,
her precious gift from God
My Mom
Who was there for me when I uttered my very first words
My Mom
I held onto the hem of her dress to keep her in my sight
Simply being near Mom caused my world to look so bright
I wanted the protection of my Mom's love always around me
I took my first steps and tried to be brave and strong you see
When I reached the age to play a little more on my own
I felt so comfortable, safe, and secure near my Mom at home
As I grew and became a little older, about 2 years of age
I had to share with three older siblings already on the stage
As time passed there were three more added to the family
That made me most special, the one in the middle, you see
I certainly had the best of both worlds, yes, I might add
Simply enjoyed being with the young and all the fun they had
I was so intrigued, sharing the special privileges with the old
Life was so exciting, adventurous, we became so very bold

Watch, stand fast in the faith, be brave, be strong.

I Corinthians 16:13

Let all that you do be done with love.

I Corinthians 16:14

Now Is the Time

Today

Today, live in peace because life has just begun
Anything you put your hands to, it's already done
Trust the Holy Spirit now to lead and guide you
You will be taught and shown just what to do
Don't put off until tomorrow what can be done today
Tomorrow is not promised, so let God have his way
The time is now, simply get on track and move on
Strive for excellence, walk or you might have to run
Help someone today, please do not let the time pass
Remember, only what you do for Christ will last
When a thought comes into your mind to give
Do it now, trust the Holy Spirit inside you and live
Always think of giving what you have, if only a dime
God will increase any amount, of course in due time
Remembering the Widow that gave her very last
Thinking, she and her son's lives would soon pass
Live peaceably, continue to trust God today
Please renew your mind, now, today is a good day

Pursue peace with all people, and holiness, without which no one will see the Lord.

Hebrews 12:14

Yes, the Lord will give what is good; And our land will yield it's increase.

Psalm 85:12

Overwhelming Sorrow

When circumstances seem to surround you
Please do not feel sad or fret, whatever you do
God is aware of all of your overwhelming sorrow
Trust, simply look forward to a better day, tomorrow
Continue to hold your head up high anyway
Remember you can make it, just love, and strive today
God will not put more on you than you can bear
Always know that the Lord sees and He is quite aware
Take heed to the word, have faith and hear
Continue to seek first and above all, have no fear
Count it all joy and simply live in peace
Believe in the Holy Spirit to get some release
Rejoice, God is working character in you
Listen, pray and be mindful of whatever you do
A little rain that falls can make you strong
Have faith, move forward, and continue to hold on
Choose your battle and yes aim to win
Believe, never waiver, all will be well in the end
You might have tears on your pillow at night
Remember that day comes in the morning light

That I have great sorrow and continual grief in my heart.

Roman 9:2

But it is good for me to draw near to God; I have put my trust in the Lord God, That I may declare all your works.

Psalm 73:28

Prayer of Thanksgiving

Lord, thank you for our lives and this beautiful day
You did not have to let us continue or see our way
Lord thank you for the peace and seeing the light
We know that it is so cozy, yet warm and very bright
Please give us the mind to be more grateful and
to always believe in you
Lord, keep us on the straight and narrow path to
enable us to stay true
If we could just reach out and touch somebody's hand
and help anyone in need
I'm sure we will be blessed and so highly favored
for doing a good deed
This is the season to give of ourselves and yes
today is a very good time
This is the season to love and share, also thankful for
a calm yet peaceful mind
Lord encourage us to begin to give from our hearts and
certainly, not from our heads
Please simply think of someone other than ourselves
and let nothing but good be said
Yes, we are now beginning to learn how important it is
to plant good seed
Thank you so much for renewing our minds and yes
awakening us to
spirit and truth indeed

Continue earnestly in prayer, being vigilant in it with thanksgiving.
Colossians 4:2

Presence of God Simply Embrace It

Woman and Your Worth

Different turns in life maybe quite sudden, are not for your downfall
Just simply a minor distraction toward your uphill climb to greatness
You are not a first or second prize, your role is critical in the equation
No longer considered an accessory or an old piece of costume jewelry
You are of great value, surely a precious and quite an elegant stone
Please know that you play a very essential part of the universe
Remember you matter whether in a friendship or special relationship
Stop losing sleep over people who disrespect or try to hurt you
That person's view of you is really quite cloudy and distorted
Know that their vision is blurred and cannot see your true worth
The crown you are wearing reveals your royalty and your heritage

- Change Is Coming -
Get ready and be prepared for that change, a special turn approaching
Slowly began to brace yourself, move into another level in your life.
My sweet Daughter it is simply called (higher level of consciousness)
All you have to do is vast in the glory and give praise to the Lord
Get ready because God is going to shower you with such blessings
He will give you the desires of your heart, just have faith to believe
Do not sit and wait, continue to go on about your Father's Business.
Don't look back at that closed door, began to sing praises to the Lord.
Began to walk in abundance and prosperity that's extended just for you
Just tell the Lord thank you for making all things new in your life
Look around, your life is already changing in the natural realm.
Know that God is working it all out for you in the spiritual realm.
Do not be afraid of unexpected changes or u- turns in your life
Remember God has everything under control, simply love and rest in Him

Began to Just Sing Out Loud　　　　　　*Victory That's My Name*
　　　　　　　　　　　　　　　　　　　Victory I Know Who I AM

But grow in the grace and knowledge of our Lord and Savior Jesus Christ.
To Him be the glory both now and forever Amen.

II Peter 3:18

Prophet, The Anointed One

Listen and Live

Prophet Elijah asked the Widow for a cup of water to drink
He also asked her to bring a little morsel of bread in her
hand, no time to think
She's saying, there is only enough meal for my son and I
If I cook the last bread and give to you, we will surely die
The widow appears to be broken, poor, suicidal, and stressed
Her life was in such turmoil, no faith, just an absolute mess
The widow began to take heed and do what he asked of her
She took the little meal, added water, and started to gently stir
There was a famine and lack spreading all over in the land
She listened to the prophet and use what was in her hand
She learned that there was a miracle in trusting and giving
Planting in good ground, now that is truly Godly living

But He said to them, why are you so fearful? How is it that you have no faith?   Mark 4:40

So she went away and did according to the word of Elijah: And she and he and her household ate for many days.   I Kings 17:15

A T that time – Barrel of Meal (Empty) and Cruise of Oil (Dry)
*   – When the little was put in the hands of the Prophet*
Cruise of Oil (Filled Up) and the Barrel of Meal (Filled Up)
Release your seed with no fear, God will Release your Harvest.

If you give to the Prophet – Barrel of Meal will never run dry.
*   -- Cruise of Oil will never run dry.*

56

 Quietness

"Speak Positive"

I would just like to say get quiet, think on what you are thinking about first
We all know that life and death is in the power of the tongue
please no more loud outburst
Be careful how you speak and what you say at any given time
Think about your thoughts, get quiet before you began to speak your mind
Purity of thoughts is quality in quietness and of course joy you must know
Please be aware that you cannot live better than what you are thinking,
that's a fact you know
You have to first began to think with a positive state of mind
and the second step is to say it
The third step in having what you say is to simply go ahead
and act on it and not just sit
If a person says that He/She does not like you for no apparent reason
In reality that person dislike themselves and is expressing
their misery toward you doing their no confidence
and low self-esteem season
So step away from the thoughts of being disliked or feeling somewhat rejected
Knowing that the other person's feelings doesn't have anything to do
with you because you are loved and is
overwhelmingly respected
Begin to believe in you and start to receive all the compliments that you get
Knowing that you are made in God's own image and He is definitely
not through with you yet
Last but not least, please do not wait on some random person
to encourage or validate you, now
Please Stand up and go ahead and Get out, Look up and yes
be quiet or maybe a little loud,
remember You Are (I AM) wow

Better a handful with quietness, than both hands full, together with toil and grasping for the wind.

Ecclesiastes 4:6

I was in the spirit on the Lord's Day, and I heard behind me a loud voice, as of a trumpet.

Revelation 1:10

Rainbow

Oh, How Beautiful

Life can be quite beautiful as a colorful rainbow
Just look at all the faces, some plain and a little glow
Some of us have lived quite a plain, pastel and others
a sequence life
Some live in the dark pouring rain either hot or cold
under and below in strife
Look up and create your own color and began to dream
Watch as the day began to look bright and highlighted
by simply creating your own scene
Be colorful and creative, make a change as you need
Look at yourself, renew your mind, trust God to succeed
Live and feel so refreshed and strive to only be you
Energize the power within and do all that you can do
When you mix colors together, that changes the tone
Just splash on the bold and the bright
the warm and the dark
you will never feel alone

I set my rainbow in the cloud; and it shall be for the sign of the covenant
between Me and the earth.

Genesis 9:13

58

Rebellious Child

Parents Never Give Up

Children obey your Mother and your Father
A rebellious child would say, why should I bother
Take time with your child today and everyday
Teach Him or Her about God's word in every way
If your child rebels and fights against you
Please do not give up on Him or Her whatever you do
A child's mind is filled with imagination and mystery
Remember you are the main part of your child's history
Continue to pray for your child always, non-stop
Seek God on the matter and not let the ball drop
Always believe that your child is safe and protected
Show your child love and to never feel rejected
Teach your child to walk in spirit and in truth
When you began to see the wonderful changes and
a complete turnaround, now that is living proof
Train up your child in the way that he or she must go
When that child departs, he or she will return joyful
and with a spirit filled glow

Children obey your parents in the Lord, for this is right.

Ephesians 6:1

I have no greater joy than to hear that my children walk in truth.

III John 1:4

Release Your Father

Work on Your Behalf (Other Side)

Your Father transitioned to be with the Lord on yesterday
I know you must began to grieve in your very own way
A Father's roll is to protect at any cost and love his child
Remembering that He was not always so meek and mild
He wanted to be there for everything in your life, you see
His job is to make good things happen for you, absolutely
He worked hard with his hands and wanted the best for you
He Pushed away all hurt, harm, danger that surrounded you
Forgive and freely release him, just breathe, and let him go
He will be there in spirit and allowing his love to show
You will feel such peace knowing, He is on the Other Side
God the Father, your Transitioned Father is working on your
behalf,
>   *true love you cannot hide*
You can only hope to win in every area of your precious life
No more feeling the pain of loss that cuts like a dull knife
You are simply covered and so overwhelmingly protected
There is no reason to feel unloved or the least bit rejected
Remember your Transitioned Father will always be with you
Know that He lives in you and is a part of whatever you do
You will no longer have thoughts of feeling scared or alone
He will forever make you feel safe and peaceful at home
Pray for peace and let your Transitioned Father gently go
Life will be better, such freedom allowing the oneness to flow

---

I and my Father are one.

John 10:30

Remain the Same

When the winds of winter come in your life
Remain the Same
When you made wrong choices and suffered the
consequences on your journey
Remain the Same
When your love one has walked away from you
When your child becomes disobedient and rebellious
toward you
Remain the Same
When you shed tears on your pillow at night
When you just could not wait for the morning light
Remain the Same
When you have read the Bible and stayed in prayer
When you have renewed your mind and kept the faith
Remain the Same
When you laughed, lived, and loved in spite of
Through it all, you have endured to the end to receive
the promise of God
Aren't you happy and so grateful that you stayed truly
focused and did not doubt in your heart
You calmly and peaceably
Remained the Same

And it may be that I will remain or even spend the winter with you, that
you may send me on my journey wherever I go.

I Corinthians 16:6

Stay in Your Own Lane

You Rule There

As you began to peel back the mask, remove the
prejudices and check your enlarged Ego
Remember thinking you are smarter than everyone
around, you know
For some reason, you think that you have all the
answers for everyone and everything
You walk up, simply take over the conversation
and just jump right into the ring
Control yourself and have a little more stability
Make a change, you truly have the capability
If you are calm and have peace on the inside
You can try harder to do better on the outside
This might be just a little difficult to hear
But it is for your own good my precious dear
Please renew your mind and think about what you do
Because in reality, the only person you can change
or makeover is you
If someone want your opinion, they will ask, so put a
hold on that superior reign
Sometimes you just have to simply stay in your own lane

Be of the same mind toward one another. Do not set your mind on high things, but associate with the humble. Do not be wise in your own opinion.
Romans 12:16

Sunshine

How Warm and Bright

Let the sun shine that gives a perfect day
Allow the sun light to guide you on your way
The bright sun shared by you and me
God gave us light to help our eyes to clearly see
May the Lord continue to bless us today
Enjoy the beautiful sun to keep us warm, we pray
Live in peace morning, noon, and night
Have faith to believe while it is still day light
See His marvelous works all day long
Move forward on your path, singing a praise song
Allow the sun to shine all over your face
Always strive to walk upright and stay in the race
The sun will purify and make all things new
Allow the brightness to shine in and through you
Please walk graciously and in a straight line
Live humble and peaceably while there is still time

But the path of the just is like the shining Sun. That shines ever Brighter unto the perfect day.

Proverb 4:18

The Lord make His face shine upon you. And be gracious to you.

Numbers 6:25

Take Time to Appreciate, Gather, Seek

Take time to Appreciate all the blessings
For we have so much to be grateful and thankful for
Take time to Forgive with a humble heart
In return, God will forgive you of your transgressions
Take time to Gather always in His name
Assemble yourselves together in the house of God
Take time to Help someone in time of need
Remember, the poor and needy will always be with us
Take time to Laugh softly and out loud
Laughter is healthy and is truly music to the soul
Take time to love and by all means be loved
For God so loved the world that He gave His Only Son
Take time to Pay your tithes and to give
Windows of Heaven will be opened, blessings poured out
Take time to Read and desire knowledge
For this is a stairway of learning and continued growth
Take time to Seek First the Kingdom of God
Just know that all will be added unto you and yours
Take time to Walk uprightly in oneness
Think inclusion, as we knock, the doors are opened to all

To everyone there is a season a time for every purpose under Heaven.

Ecclesiastes 3:1

For everyone who asks receives, and he who seeks finds, and to him who knocks it will be opened.

Matthew 7:8

Take Time to Remember

Take time to remember who you are
Always know that you are a child of the King
Take time to remember who made you
Be proud that you were created in God's own image
Take time to remember all the beauty on earth that
surrounds you
You are God's steward and care-taker of this Great land
Take time to remember to stay in covenant with God
Being in covenant is a blessing to you and your children
Take time to remember to always love
Know that God so loved the world that He gave
His only begotten Son in order for us to be free
Take time to remember that God is truly Lord of Lord
Began to remember what you have once forgotten and
to be awaken to a new and more creative you
Take time to remember to think of others
Please know when you bless others God will bless you

Genesis 1:26
And God said, let us make man in our image, after our likeness:
and let them have dominion over the fish of the sea, and over
the fowl of the air, and over the cattle, and over all the earth,
and over every creeping thing that creepeth upon the earth.

Unconditional Love

Go to the promise land that God has planned for you
Do not settle in just any place for what you need to do
Keep moving to where you're destined to be and remain
Do not stay where there is discomfort and so much pain
As you travel, walk in truth and love, not by sight
Stay on track do not lose hope, trust in God's might
Do not wait for the battle to be over start shouting now
Stand firm and stable because spirit will show you how
You might be content and at ease living in the deep pit
God is not pleased, watching you just calmly sit
You are so exhausted no more strength to stand strong
You've lost passion and drive, now that's just wrong
Seek God for your vision and bring back your sight
Night will pass, wait patiently for the morning light
You can see the abundance of the second touch
You should be so grateful and give thanks that God
        loves you without a doubt, so very much
Your passion has been restored, cleared vision and a
        renewed mind, now
Feeling so whole and so loved, no more negativity, wow

Love suffers long and is kind, love does not envy; love does not parade
itself, is not puffed up.

I Corinthians 13:4

Winter & Spring and Summer & Fall

Spring is approaching and Summer will soon be here
Everyone is so overwhelmed with laughter and cheer
The weather during night and day and is so very hot
Relax and get comfortable, just try to find a cool spot
March is a month that whirls with high and low winds
Enjoy the various seasons some I highly recommend
April is a month that is filled with rain and showers
The month of May always bring such beautiful flowers
June is thought of as a celebration month for a Bride
It is known today for its beauty, style and so much pride
You only live once and it is certainly not rehearsed
Began to breathe and enjoy being one with the universe
Continue to just be, while you are growing in grace
There is so much in your life that you will have to face
When you walk through winter, spring, summer, and fall
Sing and praise with joy, be humble and embrace all
Strive to live in harmony, stay calm, you have the ability
Be happy and think on good things without any hostility
Spring forward, strongly blossom and continue to grow
Let your light shine, such beauty as a colorful rainbow

While the earth remains, Seedtime and harvest, cold and heat, Winter, and summer; and day and night shall not cease.

Genesis 8:22

Woman and Your Worth

Rise Above Because There Is No Ashes Here

You are definitely not a bonus nor anyone's first or second prize
Know that you play a critical role in the equation, you shall rise
You are not an accessory or a piece of costume jewelry, please know
If anything, you are a precious and quite an elegant stone, let it show
You are certainly not considered to be a member of just any Team
You are an essential part of the Universe, CEO with high self-esteem.
You matter if the friendship or relationship is with a male or female.
Please know you are worth more than you realize, you shall prevail.
The most valuable player, first class, healthy and quite nourished.
When you know who you are, you will grow in grace and flourish.
No more worries or woes just began to love yourself now and always.
You are spiritual being, living a natural experience the rest of your days.
Look in the mirror and see how special and divine you really are.
Began to see your glory and how you portray a bright and shining star.
Live in the fullness of your destiny not with arrogance but with humility.
Live your life through love, not anger nor vengeance or any hostility.
Remember when you began to stand and rise to a higher height.
God will cause you to be elevated, and to shine oh so very bright.
Trust and know, you are quite extraordinary, never common, or plain
Began to step up and walk with such pride, no spots nor any stain
Never allow anyone to rule over you or attempt to validate you.
Trust God for strength, courage to accomplish whatever you desire to.
Step out of that shell that you are so comfortable resting and living in.
Grow in grace, say I'm okay, all is well and all will be well in the end.
Take another look, turn around slowly in the mirror to see the real you
You must be so amazed, look marvelous, with such poise and grace too

Began to just sing out loud – Victory that's my name
Victory I know who I Am

But grow in the grace and knowledge of our Lord and Savior Jesus Christ.
To Him be the Glory both now and forever Amen.

II Peter 3:18

Worshiper

That's Who You Are

You have a big heart and you just simply love people
You love the saved and the unsaved like a church with
or without a steeple
You love the have and the have nots, the with or
without
You believe in loving your neighbor as yourself while
you are out and about
You know who you are and do not need to be validated
If I wanted to guess who you were, I would have to say
the Son of God, you must be related
You sing the praises of God with your hands raised
You are known by your walk with God as a worshiper
and certainly by your praise
Life is an adventure, journey certainly not a destination
You want to always live in peace and of course truly
believe in restoration
You said just because you can doesn't mean you should
Always strive to live upright because you could
Do not be angry at God if you made a wrong choice
There will surely be consequences but continue to
praise God and began to rejoice

But the hour is coming and now is, when the true worshiper will worship the Father in spirit and truth; For the Father is seeking such to worship Him.

John 4:23

You

You Always
Let me know how much you love and care
You Are
All I truly need to get by in this world
You Bring
Out the best in me as I strive for excellence
You Continue
To keep me grounded and in perfect peace
You Grant
The Desires of my heart as I began to walk upright
You Have
Protected me from all the hurt harm and danger
You Just
Keep on blessing me as I travel on my journey
You Might
Not come when I want but you are always on time
You Never
Leave me or ever forsake me through it all

Yes, it is quite well with me as I walk with you

If we live in the Spirit, let us also walk in the Spirit.

Galatians 5:25

You Are Special

Not Tolerated but Celebrated

You surround yourself with people who just take from you
You are always doing something for others, not treated the
same in return that's true
When you finally notice that the friendship is not mutual no
matter how hard you try
Just step away from that situation and simply say goodbye
Take it for what it is worth and absolutely, just move on
Open your eyes, shake yourself, no longer except that
attitude or over look or condone
Remember that you are loved and is a child of the King
Please listen and by all means, do not feel as if you must
accept just anything
Renew your mind, regardless of age please know that you
are so very special
You are quite beautiful and of course God's shining vessel
Distant yourself from people who just seem to tolerate you
Make a change and associate yourself with people that
celebrate you and what you do
Do not look back, keep moving forward simply love and live
You are so unique, a person who cares and love to give
Continue to live a happy and peaceful life, enjoy, and laugh
Walking upright, God will put the right people in your path

These things I have written to you concerning those who try to deceive you.
I John 2:26

Young and Young at Heart

Read and Meditate On "Good Diet"

I. Command the Blessings
The Lord will command the blessing on you in your storehouses and in all to which you set your hand and He will bless you in the land which the Lord your God is giving you.

Deuteronomy 28:8

2. Desires of Your Heart
Delight yourself also in the Lord. And He shall give you the desires of your heart.

Psalm 37:4

3. Fruits of The Spirit
But the fruit of the Spirit is love, joy, peace, longsuffering, kindness, goodness, faithfulness, gentleness, self-control. Against such there is no law.

Galatians 5:22-23

4. Lord Give You Increase
May the Lord give you increase more and more. You and your children.

Psalm 115:14

5. No Weapon Formed
No weapon formed against you shall prosper. And every tongue which rises against you in judgment You shall condemn. This is the heritage of the servants of the Lord. And their righteousness is from Me, says the Lord.

Isaiah 54:17

6. Prosper and Health
Beloved, I pray that you may prosper in all things and be in health just as your soul prospers.

III John 1:2

7. Trust and Have Faith
Trust in the Lord, and do good; Dwell in the land, and feed on His faithfulness.

Psalm 37:3

Your Life Has Purpose

When some circumstances become difficult in your life
Look at it with an opened mind no anger or strife
Breathe very deeply because you have to go through it
The Holy Spirit will navigate give you grace please sit
There is surely and positively a lesson needed to be
            learned from it all
God will give you continued grace stay in peace stand
            strong and never fall
There is a sure blessing in that subsequent pain you feel
Trust in your inner power listen get quiet please be still
Seek to find purpose during your pain to help others
Be sensitive and encourage someone as if he/she were
            your biological sisters and brothers
Please know you are uniquely qualified to lift others up
Especially during those times when you had to drink
            from that awful bitter cup

            Remember and Know
Your Mess will absolutely become your Message
Your Pain will positively become your own Gain
Your Test will uniquely become your Testimony

In Him also we have obtained an inheritance, being predestined according
to the purpose of him who works all things according to the counsel of His
will.

Ephesians I:11

Come Back to Yourself

When you are living in the hog pen of your life
Believe you will get better without any strife
When life appears to be so difficult and hard to bare
Believe your Heavenly Father sees and does care
Moving forward on your journey each and every day
The Holy Spirit will lead and guide you along the way
Do not look at where you are in the natural right now
Your life is rapidly changing in the Spiritual realm wow
God will never leave you nor will He ever forsake you
Know whose you are continue to hold on and stay true
Get up look ahead and simply stop looking back
Open your eyes to see there is absolutely no lack
Keep the faith and always stay positive as you travel
Look at all the negative began to fall away and unravel
Simply get back your zest and began to laugh and smile
Come back to yourself without feeling you are on trial

What then shall we say to these things? If God is for us who can be against us.

Roman 8:31

Made in the USA
Charleston, SC
14 February 2017